Animals and Their Babies

Chloe Morrison

ROSEN
COMMON CORE
READERS

Rosen Classroom™

New York

Published in 2013 by The Rosen Publishing Group, Inc.
29 East 21st Street, New York, NY 10010

Book Design: Michael Harmon

Photo Credits: Cover Mark Bridger/Shutterstock.com; p. 5 smereka/Shutterstock.com;
p. 7 DKPugh/Shutterstock.com; p. 9 John Hoffman/Shutterstock.com;
p. 11 (duckling) Brian Guest/Shutterstock.com; p. 11 (flying ducks) Whytock/Shutterstock.com;
p. 13 InavanHateren/Shutterstock.com; p. 15 Karel Gallas/Shutterstock.com.

ISBN: 978-1-4488-8704-0
6-pack ISBN: 978-1-4488-8705-7

Manufactured in the United States of America

CPSIA Compliance Information: Batch #WS12RC: For further information contact Rosen Publishing, New York, New York at 1-800-237-9932.

Word Count: 52

Contents

A horse is tall.
A foal is short.

A cow is large.
A calf is little.

A lion has big paws.
A cub has small paws.

A bird flies.
A chick walks.

A pig has a long tail.
A piglet has a short tail.

A sheep is big.
A lamb is small.

Words to Know

chick

foal

paws

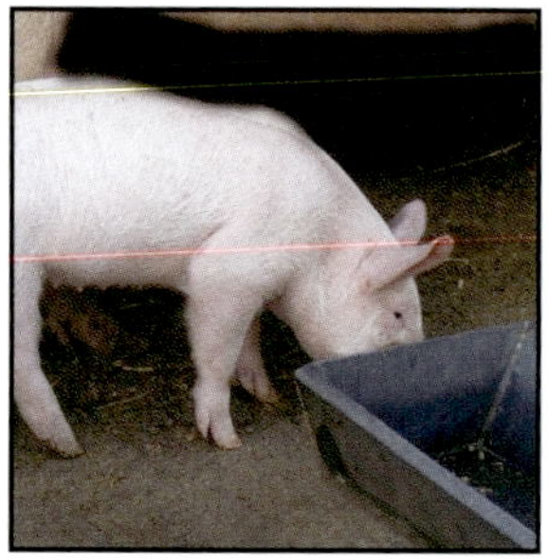

piglet

Index